JAPANESE IN AMERICA

web enhanced at **www.inamericabooks.com**

Margaret J. Goldstein

LERNER PUBLICATIONS COMPANY / MINNEAPOLIS

Current information and statistics quickly become out of date. That's why we developed **www.inamericabooks.com**, a companion website to the **In America** series. The site offers lots of additional information—downloadable photos and maps and up-to-date facts through links to additional websites. Each link has been carefully selected by researchers at Lerner Publishing Group and is regularly reviewed and updated. However, Lerner Publishing Group is not responsible for the accuracy or suitability of material on websites that are not maintained directly by us. It is recommended that students using the Internet be supervised by a parent, a librarian, a teacher, or another adult.

Lerner Publications Company
A division of Lerner Publishing Group
241 First Avenue North
Minneapolis, MN 55401 U.S.A.

Website address: www.lernerbooks.com

Library of Congress Cataloging-in-Publication Data

Goldstein, Margaret J.
    Japanese in America / by Margaret J. Goldstein.
        p.   cm. — (In America)
    Includes bibliographical references and index.
    ISBN-13: 978-0-8225-3952-0 (lib. bdg. : alk. paper)
    ISBN-10: 0-8225-3952-7 (lib. bdg. : alk. paper)
    1. Japanese Americans—History—Juvenile literature. 2. Immigrants—United States—History—Juvenile literature. 3. Japanese Americans—Juvenile literature. 4. Immigrants—United States—Juvenile literature. I. Title. II. Series: In America (Minneapolis, Minn.)
E184.J3G65 2006
973'.04956—dc22   2005017216

Manufactured in the United States of America
1 2 3 4 5 6 – JR – 11 10 09 08 07 06

CONTENTS

INTRODUCTION

In America, a walk down a city street can seem like a walk through many lands. Grocery stores sell international foods. Shops offer products from around the world. People strolling past may speak foreign languages. This unique blend of cultures is the result of America's history as a nation of immigrants.

Native peoples have lived in North America for centuries. The next settlers were the Vikings. In about A.D. 1000, they sailed from Scandinavia to lands that would become Canada, Greenland, and Iceland. In 1492 the Italian navigator Christopher Columbus landed in the Americas, and more European explorers arrived during the 1500s. In the 1600s, British settlers formed colonies that, after the Revolutionary War (1775–1783), would become the United States. And in the mid-1800s, a great wave of immigration brought millions of new arrivals to the young country.

Immigrants have many different reasons for leaving home. They may leave to escape poverty, war, or harsh governments. They may want better living conditions for themselves and their children. Throughout its history, America has been known as a nation that offers many opportunities. For this reason, many immigrants come to America.

Moving to a new country is not easy. It can mean making a long, difficult journey. It means leaving home and starting over in an unfamiliar place. But it also means using skill, talent, and determination to build a new life. The In America series tells the story of immigration to the United States and the search for fresh beginnings in a new country—in America.

JAPANESE IN AMERICA

Immigrants have come to the United States from every country on earth, including Japan, a small island nation in the Pacific Ocean. The first Japanese immigrants arrived in the United States in the late 1800s. They settled on the West Coast, where they primarily worked in farming, fishing, and business. Compared to other immigrant groups, their numbers were small. But like other immigrants, Japanese Americans tended to live near one another. They formed clubs and businesses that kept them connected to one another and to their homeland.

Also, like other immigrant groups, the Japanese faced discrimination in the United States. For the Japanese, this discrimination was particularly harsh. During World War II (1939–1945), the United States and Japan were enemies. Fearing that Japanese Americans might be disloyal, the U.S. government evacuated (removed from their communities) most Americans of Japanese descent. They had to live in remote camps for much of the war. Known as evacuees, the Japanese Americans lost their homes, businesses, and freedom.

Many years after the war, the U.S. government apologized to Japanese Americans for this injustice. By the late 1900s, as World War II faded into history, Japanese Americans were no longer treated like outcasts in their own nation. They held important roles in U.S. government, the arts, sports, technology, and business.

According to the 2000 U.S. census, approximately 1.2 million Americans are of Japanese descent, with at least one Japanese ancestor. Many of these Japanese Americans have never lived in or even visited Japan. Yet they still cherish their Japanese roots. As Japanese Americans, they embody the richness of both Japan and the United States.

ACROSS THE PACIFIC

The Asian nation of Japan is composed of four large islands and thousands of smaller islands. They sit in the Pacific Ocean, off the coast of mainland Asia. The four major islands extend for about twelve hundred miles from north to south. The largest island is Honshu, followed in size by Hokkaido, Kyushu, and Shikoku. Altogether, the Japanese islands are home to about 127 million people.

People have lived on the Japanese islands for more than thirty thousand years. The first inhabitants were Stone Age hunter–gatherers. Over the centuries, Japanese people settled into villages and planted crops. They sometimes interacted with people from China and Korea— nearby nations on mainland Asia. They learned how to make metal tools and weapons, and they developed farming techniques such as irrigation—a method of transporting water to crops.

In the A.D. 600s, on the island of Honshu, various clans (large family groups) began to fight one another for power. Eventually, one family became dominant. Its leader, Kotoku, became Japan's first emperor. He claimed to be descended from Amaterasu, the Japanese sun goddess.

The new emperor created a central Japanese government, with its capital in the city of Kyoto. Under the new government, Japanese cities grew larger and farms became more organized and efficient. The central government remained in control for several centuries.

Minamoto Yoritomo (below) *was Japan's first shogun (great general). The shogunate style of government remained in place in Japan until the late 1800s.*

Gradually, some Japanese clans grew wealthy and powerful. They lived on large private estates and hired armies of samurai, or professional warriors. These clans threatened the emperor's power. In the late 1100s, a clan named Minamoto set up its own military-style government in the town of Kamakura. With his own control weakened, the emperor agreed to share power with this clan. He gave its leader, Yoritomo, the title of shogun, or "great general." The new military government was called a shogunate.

For the next three hundred years, the shogunate changed hands several times, as different families battled one another for power. By the 1500s, Japan was awash in civil war. The nation had no clear leader. Samurai warlords fought one another for territory. The emperor remained the symbolic head of Japan, but in reality he had little power.

TO LEARN MORE ABOUT EARLY JAPANESE HISTORY, INCLUDING INFORMATION ABOUT SHOGUNS AND SAMURAI, VISIT WWW.INAMERICABOOKS.COM FOR LINKS.

EAST AND WEST

Until the 1500s, no Westerners (non–Asians) visited Japan. But in 1549, a Portuguese priest named Francis Xavier arrived in Japan. Xavier was a missionary, or religious teacher, who wanted to convert the Japanese and other Asian people to Christianity. The Japanese practiced their own ancient religions—Buddhism and Shintoism. Most Japanese were not interested in

In this painting, a family visits a Shinto temple. Shinto is Japan's oldest religion and means "the way of the gods."

Xavier's teachings. However, Xavier worked with Portuguese traders, who wanted to sell guns and other manufactured items in Asia. With Xavier's help, the Japanese began to purchase weapons and other goods from the Portuguese.

Aided by powerful new Western weapons, samurai armies continued to battle one another in Japan. Finally, in 1603, a noble named Tokugawa Ieyasu became shogun. He established a stable government and brought a degree of peace to Japan.

By then more foreign traders were doing business in Japan. They came from Spain, England, Holland, and China. Tokugawa did not like foreigners, especially those who practiced Christianity. He also wanted to make sure that Japanese nobles didn't grow too rich from international trade. Therefore, in the 1630s, he expelled most foreigners from Japan. Only a small number of Dutch and Chinese traders were allowed to continue doing business there. Japanese people were forbidden to travel abroad. Tokugawa's actions thrust Japan into a period of almost complete isolation from the rest of the world.

For more than two centuries, the Tokugawa Shogunate retained its control in Japan. Few outsiders visited Japan, and few Japanese visited other nations. However, sometimes Japanese fishing boats were damaged at sea. Unable to sail back to port, some boats drifted east across the Pacific Ocean, carried by an ocean current called the Kuroshiwo. In this way, several Japanese sailors ended up on the western coast of North America. Rescued by foreign vessels, the sailors generally caught ships back to Japan. But a few stayed in the United States, attending school and working before eventually returning home.

THE OPENING OF JAPAN

By the 1840s, the Dutch were the only Europeans trading with Japan. Other European nations, as well as the United States, were eager to do the same. These nations were interested in financial opportunities. They also wanted their merchant and whaling ships to be able to use Japanese ports for loading up on fuel and supplies.

In July 1853, Commodore Matthew C. Perry, a U.S. naval officer, arrived in Edo Bay (modern–day Tokyo Bay) with a group of heavily armed U.S. warships. With orders from U.S. president Millard Fillmore, Perry demanded that the Japanese government do business with the United States. Then he sailed away, promising to return the following spring to hear the answer to his proposal. When Perry returned, he came with even more warships.

The Tokugawa Shogunate realized that it was no match for the might of the U.S. Navy. So it agreed to U.S. demands. In 1854 Japan and the United States signed the Treaty of Kanagawa, which established political ties between the two countries. Four years later, the two nations signed a major trade agreement. Japan's long period of isolation ended. Afterward, in 1866, the Japanese government began

Commodore Matthew Perry meets with Japan's imperial commissioner in 1853.

RUSSIA
CHINA
Hokkaido
NORTH KOREA
Sea of Japan
SOUTH KOREA
JAPAN
East China Sea
Honshu
Tokyo
Kamakura
Okayama City
Osaka
Korea Strait
Tokyo Bay
Shikoku
Kyushu
NORTH PACIFIC OCEAN
RYUKYU ISLANDS
Okinawa
N

The Japanese call their country Nihon or Nippon, which means "Land of the Rising Sun." Download this and other maps at www.inamericabooks.com.

issuing passports that allowed Japanese people to travel out of the country legally.

Some Japanese people, especially military leaders, were unhappy with the Tokugawa Shogunate. They thought the treaties with the United States were a bad deal for Japan. They wanted to make their nation stronger, so it could stand up to the United States and European countries. In 1867 a group of militants overthrew the Tokugawa Shogunate. The rebels reinstalled the imperial family (the emperor's family) to supreme power. A fourteen-year-old boy named Mutsuhito became Japan's emperor. The young emperor took a new title, Meiji, meaning "enlightened rule."

Mutsuhito (above, ca. 1904) *and the other leaders of the Meiji era wanted to strengthen their nation in order to better compete with Western powers.*

The new Meiji government was eager to turn Japan into a more modern, industrialized nation. The government opened factories to produce weapons and machinery. It built roads, schools, and communications networks and strengthened its army and navy. Previously, the Japanese government had rejected Christian missionaries. But the Meiji government welcomed the missionaries as an important link to the industrialized nations of the West. Missionaries were again allowed to work in Japan, and many Japanese people converted to Christianity as a result.

THE FIRST ARRIVALS

With the creation of the Meiji government, small numbers of Japanese people began traveling to the United States. Some were students. The Japanese government sent them to the United States to learn about Western technology, government, and business. With their expenses paid by Japan, these students attended prestigious U.S. universities such as Harvard and Yale. After graduation, they returned to Japan and applied their new skills to modernizing Japanese society. Other Japanese students traveled to the United States at their own expense. To pay for their schooling and living costs, many took jobs as household servants. Most lived and studied on the West Coast, near their ports of arrival, in cities such as San Francisco and Seattle. Many of these students returned to work in Japan after graduation. But others stayed in the United States and opened their own businesses.

Some well–off Japanese people left for the United States because they were unhappy with life in Japan.

Many Japanese immigrants opened their own businesses in their new homeland. The store below, in Honolulu, Hawaii, operated in the early 1900s.

With the rise of the Meiji government, many rulers and nobles lost power and wealth. Some of them strongly opposed the new government. But rather than stay and fight the new leaders, they chose to make a new start in the United States.

Some early Japanese migrants were poor laborers. Of this group, many did not move to the United States itself. Instead they moved to the Hawaiian Islands, where they labored on U.S.-owned sugar plantations.

INCREASED MIGRATION

In the 1890s, Japanese immigration to the United States picked up speed. Each year during the decade, the number of Japanese entering the United States increased by about one thousand over the previous year's number. In 1900 more than ten thousand Japanese people entered the United States.

Economic conditions in Japan fueled this increase. In Japan taxes were high and farmland was expensive. The nation frequently

suffered from poor harvests, which forced many farmers into poverty. Jobs in construction, industry, and domestic (home) service were extremely low paying.

In the face of a bleak future, many single, young Japanese men left their nation for the United States. Many of these migrants were

I happened to see a Western movie, called **Rodeo,** *at the Golden Horse Theater in Okayama City, and was completely obsessed with "American fever.". . . Enormous continent! Rich land! One could see a thousand miles at a glance! Respect for freedom and equality! That must be my permanent home, I decided.*

—Frank Tomori, recalling his decision to leave Japan for the United States younger sons, who were not due to inherit any land from their parents. (In Japan the eldest son typically inherited family land.) Most of them did not plan to stay in the United States long. They hoped to work for a few years, build up a nest egg (savings account), and then return to Japan to buy their own land or pursue business ventures.

Many early migrants did return home to Japan. They told stories of great opportunities in the United States. They reported that land was cheap, jobs were plentiful, and a bright young man could make a fortune there.

TO DISCOVER SOME OF THE MANY STORIES OF JAPANESE MIGRATING TO THE UNITED STATES, VISIT WWW.INAMERICABOOKS.COM FOR LINKS.

Inspired by these stories, immigrants saved or borrowed money to pay for their passage across the Pacific. They had to receive permission from the Japanese government to leave. Once approved, they traveled by ship, usually alongside immigrants from other Asian countries. They slept below deck, crowded together into rows of bunk beds. The food was stale and sometimes rotten. Bathroom areas were dirty. Disease sometimes swept through the ships. Depending on the weather, the trip across the Pacific took about three weeks.

Upon arriving in U.S. ports, immigrants entered buildings called processing stations. There, U.S. officials examined their identification documents and gave them medical tests. Japanese immigrants were usually in good health and had their papers in order, because the Japanese government also screened immigrants before they left Japan. But immigrants who had gotten sick on board ship were often quarantined, or isolated, in special hospitals. The sickest were denied entry into the United States.

Once through the processing station, Japanese immigrants would seek out friends or relatives who had arrived in the United States earlier. Those who had no connections in the United States rented rooms at Japanese-owned boardinghouses and small hotels. The managers there also worked as employment agents and helped the newcomers find jobs.

Job Options

The United States did indeed offer many employment opportunities for immigrants. Some entered the fishing industry. Japan's own fleets had long fished the Pacific Ocean and the Sea of Japan, so many immigrants had fishing experience. They joined fleets that fished wide areas of the Pacific Ocean, from Central America to Hawaii. Other Japanese worked onshore in canneries—processing plants where workers cleaned fish and packed them into cans for sale. Other immigrants worked on railroads and construction sites. Many of these immigrants were contract laborers—workers whose ocean voyage, housing, and employment were all arranged and managed by a company. Those immigrants who had already learned a profession in Japan typically headed to cities, where they set up their own businesses as doctors, accountants, or merchants. Since few immigrants knew English, their customers were generally other Japanese immigrants.

Many people are interested in learning about their family's history. This study is called genealogy. If you'd like to learn about your own genealogy and how your ancestors came to America, visit www.inamericabooks.com for tips and links to help you get started. There you'll also find tips on researching names in your family history.

CONTRACT LABORERS

Some Japanese firms, called emigration companies, made a business of finding jobs in the United States for Japanese laborers. The workers were called contract laborers because they signed contracts with the companies, agreeing to certain wages and other employment terms. The companies made all the arrangements: They transported the workers by ship to the United States or Hawaii, took them by train to job sites, and supervised their labor on-site.

Many contract laborers were sent to the West Coast of the United States—usually to California, Oregon, or Washington but sometimes to Montana, Idaho, or other western states. There, they took jobs on railroads, construction sites, and farms, and in fish canneries. But the majority of contract laborers went to Hawaii, where they worked on sugar plantations. U.S. employers liked Japanese contract laborers because they would work for lower wages than U.S.-born laborers would accept. However, many U.S.-born laborers resented the Japanese for taking the available work and helping to keep wages low.

For their part, Japanese laborers were eager to take contract work because the pay, although low, was more than they could earn at home in Japan. But sometimes emigration companies cheated workers. When they reached the United States, some workers found that the jobs they had been promised didn't exist. Employers also mistreated workers. Some workers performed dangerous, backbreaking jobs for eleven hours each day. They lived in run-down, unsanitary quarters.

Fast-growing farms in the western United States needed laborers, and Japanese workers were quick to fill this need. Most of the workers came from small villages and rural areas in Japan, where farming was the chief way of earning a living, so they took easily to farmwork in the United States. After working for wages for a time, some immigrants rented farms. Those who could save enough money bought their own farms. Soon Japanese people were running successful farms in many parts of the West Coast, especially California.

Many Japanese farmers in the United States combined traditional farming methods from Japan with modern methods.

DURING THOSE DAYS AROUND FRESNO [CALIFORNIA], LABORERS DID NOT EVEN CARRY BLANKETS. THEY SLEPT IN THE FIELDS WITH WHAT THEY HAD ON. THEY DRANK RIVER WATER BROUGHT IN BY IRRIGATION DITCHES. . . . SLAVING AWAY FROM 4:00 A.M. TO 9:00 P.M., THIS UNHEALTHY LIFE WAS INTOLERABLE.

—description of life for Japanese contract laborers in the early 1890s

FARMING SUCCESS

Japanese American farms tended to be small—only 56 acres compared with 320 acres for the typical West Coast farm in the early 1900s. Although small, the farms were highly productive—able to grow large amounts of crops. Japanese American farmers speeded up the harvest of certain crops, delayed the growing of others, and introduced new crops, such as rice, in order to keep their farms productive year-round. They cultivated previously dusty and desert lands that earlier U.S. farmers had avoided. By using irrigation systems, the Japanese were able to turn these lands into productive fields and orchards.

Some Japanese immigrants went into the wholesale produce business. That is, they purchased large quantities of fruits and vegetables from farmers and then resold them to grocery stores and restaurants. This business got its start because non-Japanese wholesalers sometimes boycotted (refused to buy from) Japanese farmers. So other Japanese went into the wholesale business to provide an outlet for the produce of boycotted farmers. In this way, Japanese Americans gradually came to control the entire West Coast supply of certain crops (strawberries, celery, peas, and lettuce, for instance) from planting to sale.

THE GENDER GAP

In the early years of Japanese immigration to the United States, most immigrants were men between the ages of twenty and forty. Thus Japanese men greatly outnumbered Japanese women in the United States—in some places by twenty to one. Taking an American bride would have been out of the question for most Japanese men, because Japanese (and U.S.) society frowned upon racially mixed marriages. Therefore, many Japanese men in the United States sought out brides back in Japan.

The typical male Japanese immigrant did not have enough money or free time to travel to Japan to look for a bride. So a new tradition developed. It was called the picture-bride marriage. To find a wife, a young immigrant man would write a letter to his parents in Japan, telling them to look for a suitable Japanese woman—preferably a woman from his hometown. Once the man's family located a potential bride, they made extensive inquiries into the woman's family background, schooling, manners, and general character.

LIVING IN TWO WORLDS

Children of first-generation Japanese immigrants faced the challenges of growing up in two different worlds: Japanese culture and American culture. With their siblings and friends, they spoke English, but with their parents, they spoke Japanese. Some children went to U.S. public schools during the day and attended special Japanese language and culture schools at night. As teenagers, many Japanese American youths tried to better blend in to U.S. society. Some translated their Japanese names into their English equivalents. For instance, Yuriko became Lily, and Katsu became Victor. Some young people used one name at home and another in school.

The bride's relatives did the same, investigating their potential son-in-law's family, character, and financial status.

If both parties were satisfied with the match, a wedding took place in Japan. The bride was in attendance, but the groom was nearly halfway around the world. His family stood in for him at the ceremony. Both before and after the ceremony, the bride and groom would get to know each other by exchanging letters and pictures, which explains the term *picture bride*.

After the marriage ceremony, the Japanese government permitted the bride to join her new husband in the United States. Often couples had a second wedding ceremony after the woman arrived. Historians estimate that more than five thousand Japanese women came to the United States as picture brides.

When the day finally came for us to meet our husbands, we excitedly helped to dress each other in a . . . special kimono with a crest, and a fancy sash. . . . Outside the immigration station, our husbands waited eagerly for a glimpse of us. We were nervous and shy, I thought my husband was tall and handsome.

—picture bride Tatsuyo Hazama, recalling the day she met her husband in Hawaii

2 "A Dangerous Element"

Although many immigrants planned to return home to Japan after a time, plans often changed. Once they had settled into jobs or started families in the United States, Japanese immigrants began to put down roots. They grew accustomed to American life. Many ran successful farms or companies, with employees, facilities, and business connections. Returning to Japan no longer seemed appealing or realistic to them. So they abandoned plans to go home.

Like many minorities in the United States, the Japanese of the West Coast states tended to live near one another for companionship and assistance. Neighborhoods known as Japan Towns or Little Tokyos (Tokyo had become Japan's capital) sprang up in big cities on the West Coast. These neighborhoods featured Japanese restaurants and

In the early 1900s, Los Angeles's Little Tokyo was home to many successful Japanese businesses.

other Japanese-owned businesses. A strong sense of community developed among the Japanese living there. Japanese-language newspapers helped the immigrants stay connected to one another and to their home country.

Japanese immigrants also formed a number of associations. For instance, people from certain prefectures, or regions in Japan, often formed social clubs in the United States. Members helped one another both socially and financially. Other immigrants formed religious clubs for Japanese Americans who practiced Buddhism, Shintoism, or Christianity. Many Japanese American farmers formed associations to promote and protect their business interests. The Japanese Association of America (JAA) was founded in 1905. It served as an umbrella group for many smaller regional groups.

OUTSIDERS IN AMERICA

While retaining their Japanese heritage, the immigrants also made great efforts to fit into U.S. society. Both men and women abandoned their traditional Japanese clothing (robes called kimonos, for instance) and adopted typical American styles. Although most Japanese practiced Buddhism or Shintoism, some practiced Christianity, the dominant religion in the United States.

In an effort to fit into their new culture, many Japanese immigrants adopted Western styles of dress.

Still, it was hard for Japanese immigrants to blend into mainstream U.S. culture. Their physical characteristics—almond-shaped eyes, dark hair, and light brown skin color—identified them as foreigners. Along with other immigrants, as well as African Americans, they often faced prejudice. In some West Coast cities, they had to sit apart from white customers in theaters. Some shops and restaurants refused to serve them. Real estate agents often refused to sell them houses.

U.S. law contributed to the discrimination. According to an 1873 law, only whites and African Americans were eligible to become citizens of the United States. Since Japanese and other Asian people weren't considered white, they were ineligible for U.S. citizenship, no matter how long they lived in the United States. (Their children born in the United States were U.S. citizens, however.) As noncitizens, Japanese immigrants were not allowed to practice law or hold public office. This barrier made it hard for the immigrants to use the U.S. legal system to fight for their rights.

Some Americans criticized the immigrants' home country of Japan. They said Japan was a militaristic, or warlike, nation. It had gone to war with Russia in 1904 and had quickly won a series of battles. Some U.S. leaders feared that Japan would try to conquer neighboring states in the Pacific region. They labeled Japanese expansion the

> *In one instance, I went to a barber shop to get my hair trimmed. On entering the shop, one of the barbers approached me and asked for my nationality. I answered that I was Japanese, and as soon as he heard [this], he drove me out of the place as if he were driving away a cat or a dog.*
>
> *—Japanese immigrant, recalling racial discrimination*

"yellow peril"—a reference to the so-called yellow skin color of Japanese people. At the same time, many non-Asian Americans felt threatened by the Japanese in the United States. Some critics said that Japanese Americans were loyal not to the United States but to the Meiji emperor of Japan.

Some of the worst anti-Japanese hostility emerged in San Francisco in the first decade of the 1900s. The city's labor unions (groups that fought for the rights of workers) were angry that Japanese immigrants in the railroad, construction, and other industries would work for low wages. Because it was cheaper to hire Japanese workers, some employers were eager to hire them instead of non-Japanese workers. Union leaders charged that Japanese workers were driving other Americans out of their jobs.

With the backing of the *San Francisco Chronicle*, the city's leading newspaper, labor unions began an all-out attack against Japanese Americans. Labor leaders announced a citywide boycott against Japanese American merchants. At mass meetings, white Americans called Japanese immigrants intruders who were undermining the values of the United States. Some white Americans physically assaulted Japanese immigrants.

The anti-Japanese forces demanded that the federal government prohibit further Japanese immigration into the United States. California lawmakers introduced such a bill in Congress. President Theodore Roosevelt did not want to offend the Japanese government. He spoke out against the bill, and the issue died down for a time.

Then, on April 18, 1906, a devastating earthquake hit San Francisco. Fires swept through many neighborhoods, including San Francisco's Japan Town. More than ten thousand Japanese Americans lost their homes in the fires and had to find new places to live. Some moved into neighborhoods that had previously been all white. Angered by the influx of Japanese people into their neighborhoods, many white Americans looted Japanese-owned stores and hurled abuse at Japanese Americans.

Later in 1906, the San Francisco school board ruled that Japanese American students could no longer go to school with students of European descent. The board claimed that city schools were overcrowded, and it directed all

Smoke from multiple fires billows into the sky following the 1906 earthquake in San Francisco. The fires burned unchecked for three days. The disaster left 28,000 buildings in ruins, 250,000 people homeless, and 3,000 dead.

children of Japanese immigrants to attend a separate "Oriental school" in San Francisco's Chinatown (Chinese neighborhood). Japanese Americans immediately protested this order. They noted that attending the school would be extremely difficult for Japanese children, many of whom lived far from Chinatown. More important, Japanese families were angered by the order, which was clearly based on discrimination. The school board had cited overcrowding as its reason for moving the students. But out of twenty-five thousand students in the San Francisco schools, fewer than one hundred were Japanese American. The Japanese government also protested the order. President Roosevelt again came to the support of the Japanese community and spoke out against the board's action.

The school board agreed to reverse the order, but President Roosevelt felt pressured to give in to some demands of the anti-Japanese forces. Roosevelt asked the Japanese government to limit immigration to only skilled Japanese workers and to the relatives (including picture brides) of immigrants already living in the United States. Japan agreed. The arrangement was called the Gentlemen's Agreement because it was simply an understanding between the two governments. It was not a formal treaty and was never put into writing. Japan cooperated with the agreement, and immigration numbers fell significantly.

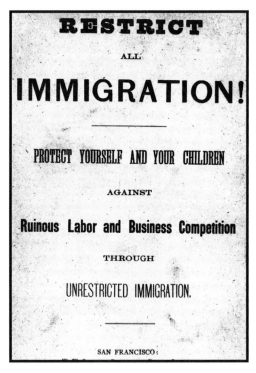

With immigration on the rise in the late 1800s and early 1900s, anti-immigration posters such as this one expressed open hostility toward newcomers.

For a while, violence and anger against Japanese Americans died down. But as Japanese American farmers in California grew more successful, non-Japanese farmers grew worried and resentful. They believed that Japanese American farmers were undermining their success. Farm organizations demanded that Japanese immigrants not be allowed to acquire more farmland in California.

The California legislature responded by overwhelmingly passing the Alien Land Law of 1913. This law banned the purchasing of farmland by anyone who was not eligible for U.S. citizenship. Such wording targeted Japanese immigrants (who were ineligible because they were not "white") without mentioning them specifically. The law also limited the length of Japanese-held land leases (rental agreements) to three years.

Japanese immigrants protested, but their protests were generally ignored. Unable to change the law, the Japanese found ways around it. For example, those who had U.S.-born children could buy property in the names of their children, who were U.S. citizens.

CLOSING THE DOOR ON IMMIGRATION

By 1920 approximately 110,000 Japanese people lived on the U.S. mainland, about 65 percent of them in California. About one-quarter of these people were U.S. citizens by birth (the children of first-generation immigrants). The Japanese on the mainland made up

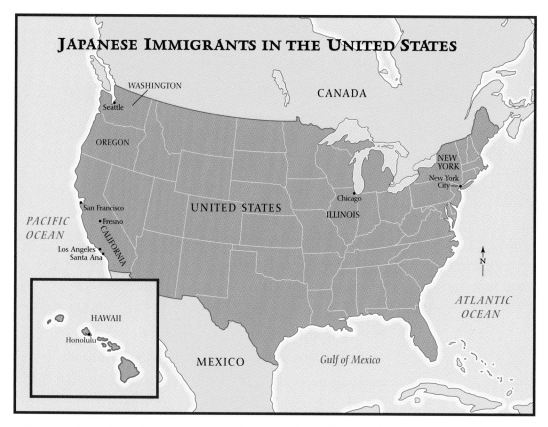

JAPANESE IMMIGRANTS IN THE UNITED STATES

WASHINGTON

Seattle

OREGON

San Francisco

Fresno

CALIFORNIA

Los Angeles

Santa Ana

PACIFIC OCEAN

UNITED STATES

CANADA

NEW YORK

New York City

Chicago

ILLINOIS

ATLANTIC OCEAN

N

HAWAII

Honolulu

MEXICO

Gulf of Mexico

Japanese have formed strong communities throughout the United States. Visit www.inamericabooks.com to download this and other maps.

a tiny proportion of the overall population. But on the Hawaiian Islands, which had become a U.S. territory in 1900, Japanese immigrants made up a much larger percentage of the population. In 1920 nearly 48 percent of Hawaii's citizens were Japanese Americans.

Discrimination against people of Japanese descent continued. In California in 1920, the state legislature enacted an even stricter alien land law, closing the loopholes in the 1913 law that had enabled the children of Japanese immigrants to buy land. In 1921 the state of Washington followed with its own legal restrictions on land ownership by Japanese Americans. Also in 1921, pressured by the U.S. government, Japan agreed to stop picture-bride emigration, in an arrangement nicknamed the Ladies' Agreement.

The final success of the anti-Japanese forces on the West Coast came when the U.S. Congress passed the Immigration Act of 1924. Without mentioning the Japanese by name, this law provided for their total exclusion by refusing entry to immigrants who were ineligible for U.S. citizenship. President Calvin Coolidge signed the act into law. Although the U.S. government still permitted a few Japanese people to enter for family reasons or under other unusual circumstances, Japanese immigration to the United States came to a virtual halt.

THE COMING OF WAR

As the United States and other nations had feared, Japan embarked on a policy of expansion in the Pacific. In 1931 Japan invaded Manchuria, a northeastern province of China. The United States and many other nations denounced the invasion. In 1934 Japan withdrew from an international peacekeeping association called the League of Nations and scrapped an international treaty limiting the size of its navy. In 1937 Japan launched a major attack on China.

Japanese military actions caused anti-Japanese sentiment to rise rapidly in the United States. Soon the U.S. government stopped oil shipments to Japan. Relations between the two nations steadily worsened.

In 1939 World War II started in Europe. The war pitted the Axis powers—led at first by Germany and Italy—against the Allied powers, led at the time by

France and Great Britain. In 1940 Japan joined the Axis powers. It continued its expansion in the Pacific, invading French Indochina (part of Southeast Asia) in September 1940.

As Japanese aggression continued, anti-Japanese voices in the United States grew louder. They attacked Japanese Americans for unfair job competition, supposed loyalty to the Japanese emperor, and "anti-American" values.

PEARL HARBOR

On December 7, 1941, Japan made a shocking move. With a fleet of bombers, it attacked the U.S. naval base at Pearl Harbor in Hawaii, destroying much of

The USS Arizona *burns after Japan's attack on Pearl Harbor, Hawaii.*

the U.S. Pacific Fleet and killing and wounding several thousand U.S. troops and civilians. Immediately, the United States declared war on Japan. In response, Germany declared war on the United States. Thus the United States entered World War II. It sent troops to battlefields in both Europe and the Pacific.

With U.S. entry into the war, anti-Japanese sentiment in the United States reached a new level. Rumors circulated that thousands of Japanese Americans were actually Japanese spies. One story said that Japanese Americans in Hawaii had assisted in the attack on Pearl Harbor by flashing light signals, sending radio transmissions, and even mowing their crop fields in the shape of arrows to point Japanese bombers toward Pearl Harbor. Another rumor said that Japanese

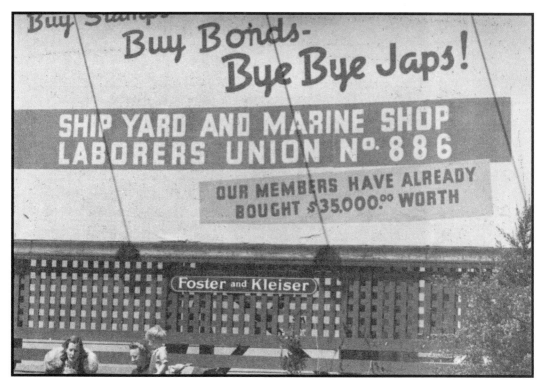

Anti-Japanese sentiment was stronger than ever after the 1941 bombing of Pearl Harbor, as seen on this billboard.

American fishing fleets in Hawaii were spying on U.S. naval ships.

Soon, throughout the American West, farm groups, veterans' organizations, patriotic associations, and business organizations were demanding that all Japanese Americans be sent to prison camps or expelled from the United States altogether. California took away the business licenses of five thousand Japanese immigrants. The U.S. government arrested about fifteen hundred other Japanese Americans as suspected spies. Earl Warren, California's attorney general, argued that all Japanese American associations should be broken up and that Japanese American farms near U.S. naval, army, and air force bases should be shut down. One military report said that "the Japanese population [is] ideally situated to carry into execution a tremendous program of sabotage [betrayal] on a mass scale."

Frightened and assaulted from every direction, Japanese Americans tried to prove their loyalty to the United States. One group of Japanese Americans in Santa Ana, California, donated money to purchase an antiaircraft gun for the U.S. military. Thousands rushed to join the Japanese American Citizens League (JACL), a patriotic organization begun by second-generation Japanese Americans. But such efforts did no good. The forces allied against them were too great. Radio shows and newspapers spewed out hateful words, calling

After the Pearl Harbor bombing, the Japanese American owner of this Oakland, California, store posted a sign to the front of his store to prove his loyalty to the United States.

Japanese Americans "a dangerous element" and a threat to U.S. security. Vandals scrawled racial slurs across Japanese American homes and storefronts. One newspaper columnist wrote:

> Everywhere that the Japanese have attacked to date, the Japanese population has risen to aid the attackers.... What is there to make the Government believe that the same wouldn't be true in California.... I am for the immediate removal of every Japanese on the West Coast [to] a point deep in the interior. Herd 'em up, pack 'em off and give 'em the inside room in the Badlands. Let 'em be pinched, hurt, hungry and dead up against it.

At the national level, U.S. government officials were divided about how to deal with Japanese Americans. Many in the government did not see them as a threat, but others insisted that they be imprisoned in camps until the end of the war. Ultimately, the anti-Japanese forces won out. On February 19, 1942, President Franklin D. Roosevelt signed Executive Order 9066, authorizing the U.S. military to move "any or all persons" out of strategic military territory. The War Department (the present-day Department of Defense) used this order to justify the transfer of all Japanese Americans to relocation camps. An organization called the War Relocation Authority (WRA) was put in charge of evacuating and housing Japanese Americans.

NOW THEREFORE . . . I authorize and direct the Secretary of War . . . to prescribe [designate] military areas in such places and of such extent as he or the appropriate Military Commanders may determine, from which any or all persons may be excluded.

—excerpt from Executive Order 9066

EXILES IN THEIR OWN LAND

At the time of Executive Order 9066, about 110,000 Japanese Americans were living in California, Oregon, and Washington. Approximately 10,000 more Japanese Americans lived in other states. All of them—citizens and noncitizens alike—were ordered to move to relocation camps. More than half of the evacuees were children. More than 65 percent were U.S. citizens. The only Japanese Americans exempt from the order were those living in Hawaii. Because Japanese Americans made up such a large percentage of the Hawaiian population, moving them to camps seemed unrealistic.

WRA officials usually gave Japanese families a few weeks—but sometimes as little as three days—to prepare to leave their homes. Officials told families to pack only bedding, clothing, kitchen utensils, and toilet items. Everything else had to be sold, stored, or abandoned. In their haste, many Japanese American business owners sold their merchandise for only a fraction of its true value. Many farmers left their crops standing in the fields and sold their equipment for

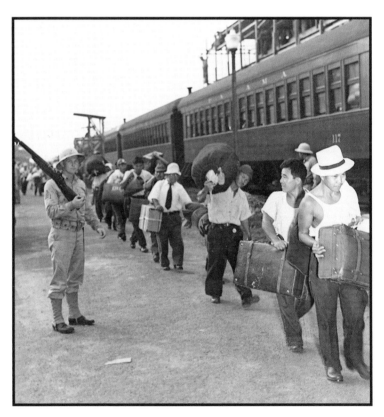

A group of Japanese men board a train bound for a relocation camp in 1942.

WE ARE GOING INTO EXILE AS OUR DUTY TO OUR COUNTRY BECAUSE THE PRESIDENT AND MILITARY COMMANDER OF THE AREA HAVE DEEMED IT A NECESSITY. WE ARE GLADLY COOPERATING BECAUSE THIS IS ONE WAY OF SHOWING . . . OUR LOYALTY.

—Saburo Kido, president of the Japanese American Citizens League

only a few dollars. Fishers also sold their boats for rock–bottom prices. Some families rented out their homes, sold them quickly, or simply left them sitting empty.

Although a few Japanese Americans tried to resist or protest the order, most dutifully obeyed it. By cooperating with WRA officials, they hoped again to prove that they were loyal U.S. citizens.

First, evacuees traveled by bus or train to one of sixteen temporary camps, or assembly centers, set up at racetracks, fairgrounds, and other large facilities. At the same time, the government rushed to construct ten permanent WRA camps, eight of them in western states and two in Arkansas. After several months at temporary camps, evacuees headed to the permanent camps by train.

The camps were located on remote public lands in desolate areas. Many camps were in the desert. Each camp was designed to house about ten thousand people and contained about a dozen

barracks, or housing units, where families lived in small rooms and slept on army–style cots. Everyone ate together in large mess halls, and they shared toilet facilities.

Children went to school at the camps. Camp authorities assigned

The desert was bad enough. The constant . . . storms loaded with sand and dust made it worse. After living in well furnished homes with every modern convenience and suddenly [being] forced to live the life of a dog is something which one cannot easily forget. . . . We were showered with dust. We slept in the dust; we breathed the dust; and we ate the dust.

—WRA evacuee, recalling conditions at the Manzanar camp in eastern California

Japanese Americans kept busy at the relocation camps. These women at the Topaz War Relocation Center in Topaz, Utah, are sewing a flag.

some adults to paid jobs, such as camp maintenance, clerical work, assembling goods for the military, and preparing food. Other adults irrigated and farmed land and tended livestock near the camps. Armed guards in watchtowers made sure that no one left camp without authorization.

Despite being forced from their homes and thrown together in close quarters with strangers, the Japanese American population did its best to make camp life tolerable. Evacuees organized recreational activities and printed camp newspapers. The WRA allowed them to elect camp councils, committees that represented the evacuees' concerns to camp authorities.

A Different War

In the first year after Pearl Harbor, the government would not allow Japanese Americans to join the U.S. military. Some Japanese Americans who were already serving in the military were discharged (kicked out). But some evacuees wanted to prove their loyalty to the United States, and the military desperately needed fighters. So in early 1943, the U.S. government announced a new policy. It allowed military-age men in relocation camps to join the U.S. Army. About twelve hundred men signed up, eager both to leave the camps and fight for the United States.

LANGUAGE EXPERTS

While the United States was fighting in Europe, it also battled Japanese troops in the Pacific. The military needed Japanese language speakers to interpret and translate enemy messages and to question prisoners. Since few non–Japanese Americans could speak or read Japanese, Japanese Americans were the obvious choice for this job. In addition to interpreters and translators *(right)*, some Japanese Americans became instructors at military language schools, where they trained other soldiers to speak and read Japanese.

(Later in the war, some men in relocation camps were drafted, or required to join the military.) The new soldiers were assigned to an all–Japanese American combat unit, the 442nd Regimental Combat Team.

Another all–Japanese American combat unit, the 100th Infantry Battalion, was formed from Japanese American members of the Hawaiian National Guard. In September 1943, the 100th arrived on the battlefields of Italy. For six months, the battalion saw constant and heavy fighting. The unit suffered almost six hundred casualties (soldiers killed or wounded) during the Italian campaign.

The 442nd Regimental Combat Team arrived in Italy in June 1944 and absorbed the 100th Infantry Battalion into its ranks. In October 1944, the unit

Members of the 100th Infantry Battalion march in Italy in May 1944.

performed its most heroic action—the rescue of the famous "Lost Battalion." The Lost Battalion was a group of Texas soldiers trapped behind German lines. The campaign took six days and cost many American lives, but the mission was successful. By war's end, the 442nd proved to be the most highly decorated unit in U.S. military history. Its soldiers had earned 18,143 Medals of Valor and 9,486 Purple Hearts.

THE END OF RELOCATION

Back at home, WRA administrators realized that keeping thousands of Americans locked up was a waste of human resources and talent—especially in wartime, when every able-bodied person was needed for the war effort. The WRA decided to allow some evacuees to leave the camps and contribute to wartime work. It sent some college-age evacuees to universities. It sent groups of other evacuees to work on distant farms, which desperately needed laborers. Some evacuees took jobs in towns and cities throughout the United States.

FIND LINKS TO MORE INFORMATION ABOUT WORLD WAR II AND JAPANESE INTERNMENT CAMPS AT WWW.INAMERICABOOKS.COM.

Since the war was still in progress, the WRA did not send any evacuees back to the West Coast—still considered a strategic military zone. Instead, most of the workers went to cities and farms in the Midwest. They faced some discrimination in their new communities, but anti-Japanese sentiment was not as strong farther east as it was in the western states.

As more and more Japanese left the camps, some former evacuees began lawsuits against the

U.S. government. They charged that the evacuation of Japanese Americans was illegal. The JACL, which had shut down during the first few years of the war, reopened its offices in many U.S. cities. The JACL joined in the legal battles against evacuation and relocation.

Eventually, some of the lawsuits reached the U.S. Supreme Court. In 1944 the court ruled that the evacuation of certain people in wartime was legal. But in a later decision, the court ruled that the United States had no right to hold loyal Americans in prison. Soon afterward, the WRA announced that all camps would be closed by the end of 1945. One-by-one, the camps shut down, and groups of evacuees departed by train or bus. Japan formally surrendered to the United States in September 1945, ending World War II in the Pacific (the European war had ended several months earlier).

NAMES AND TERMS

The U.S. government placed Japanese Americans in two different kinds of camps during World War II. Most Japanese Americans went to one of the ten well-known relocation camps. But Japanese Americans whom the government had identified as strongly "pro-Japanese" and a "threat to national security" were imprisoned in one of three lesser-known internment camps, located in North Dakota, Nebraska, and Texas. Even though relocation camps and internment camps were different, the term *internment* is often used to describe the entire World War II evacuation and relocation process.

3

RENEWAL

With the shutting of the relocation camps, the evacuees were free to go home. But many had no homes to return to. Having sold or abandoned their businesses, farms, and property on the West Coast, many chose instead to settle in the Midwest and East, in cities such as Chicago and New York. There, racism was far less severe than it was in the West. Some first-generation evacuees even chose to return to Japan after the war.

About one-third of the evacuees did move back to their old homes on the West Coast. In many cases, they found that the property they had left behind had been vandalized, neglected, or stolen.

Church, government, and humanitarian groups gave some assistance to the returnees, such as transportation and temporary housing. Even so, everyone had to start their lives over.

Happy to be home, this family was all smiles after their release from the Granada War Relocation Center in Colorado.

LEGAL BATTLES

With evacuation and relocation officially over, Japanese Americans took their struggles to the courts. They wanted to make sure that the injustices of the past were righted and were not repeated. The JACL took the lead in legal battles. The victories came fairly easily. Americans had been shocked to learn that the German government had imprisoned and murdered about six million Jews as well as millions of other Europeans during World War II. Awakened to the horrors of singling out minorities, many Americans felt shame and guilt for their own treatment of Japanese Americans during the war. In addition, the civil rights movement—the fight for equality between black and white Americans—was just beginning in the United States. As Americans developed a new sense of racial justice, barriers began to fall for Japanese Americans.

In 1945 Congress passed the War Brides Act. This law allowed U.S. servicemen to marry women they had met overseas, including Japanese women, and bring them home to live in the United States. The law overrode the earlier Ladies' Agreement, which had forbidden such a practice. Another bill, passed in June 1948, gave citizenship to any aliens (noncitizens) who had served in the U.S. armed forces during the war. This law gave citizenship to some members of the 100th and 442nd combat units.

Next, Congress created the Evacuation Claims Commission, designed to reimburse (repay) Japanese Americans for property loss caused by relocation. This law was not very effective. Former evacuees who wanted to file claims had to provide evidence to support them. Many evacuees had no documents to prove how much their lost property had been worth. Altogether, former evacuees filed nearly twenty-four thousand claims totaling approximately $132,000,000. Most individual claims were less than $5,000. But the U.S. government challenged many claims and generally paid only part of what was requested. Historians believe the government repaid less than 15 percent of the actual losses suffered by evacuees.

THE LESSONS LEARNED [ABOUT RELOCATION] MUST REMAIN AS A GRAVE REMINDER OF WHAT WE MUST NOT ALLOW TO HAPPEN AGAIN TO ANY GROUP.

—Daniel Inouye (U.S. representative, senator, and member of the 442nd Regimental Combat Team), quoted in inscription at the National Japanese American Memorial in Washington, D.C.

Many homes and businesses, such as the Buddhist temple above, were lost to vandalism during wartime relocation. Some Japanese Americans were repaid for their losses, but many were not.

Far worse than material losses, evacuees had lost their livelihoods and sense of self-worth in the camps. Many once successful farmers became low-wage gardeners after the war. Former shop owners took jobs as waiters and dishwashers. The transition was especially hard on older adults. The notion of starting over in business was unrealistic for elderly people. Many instead relied on their adult children for financial support.

A CHANGE OF ATTITUDE

One of the most important laws for Japanese Americans was the 1952 McCarran–Walter Act. This law eliminated race as a consideration in

U.S. immigration and citizenship. In other words, non-whites, including Japanese and other Asians, could finally become citizens of the United States. By 1965, after filling out the necessary paperwork and passing tests, about forty-six thousand first-generation Japanese Americans had become U.S. citizens. In many cases, people who had lived in the United States for decades were able to vote for the first time.

THE JAPANESE IN HAWAII

When Japanese immigration began in the late 1800s, Hawaii was not a U.S. state. Instead, it was an independent kingdom. However, many U.S. businesses owned land in Hawaii, and the United States had great influence over Hawaiian affairs. In 1900 Hawaii became a U.S. territory. By then thousands of Japanese immigrants were living on Hawaii. Many of them had arrived as contract laborers, working on U.S.-owned sugar plantations. By 1920 almost half of Hawaii's citizens were of Japanese descent. Immigrants from other Asian nations, as well as native Hawaiians, made up most of the rest of the population. In 1959 Hawaii became the fiftieth state in the United States. Daniel Inouye, a World War II veteran, became the new state's first congressional representative and the first Japanese American in the U.S. Congress.

In modern Hawaii, about 17 percent of the population is of Japanese descent. Although English is the state's official language, it is common to see Japanese-language magazines and newspapers there, and Japanese words appear on street signs and storefronts. Many Hawaiian students study Japanese in school.

The children of the immigrants, meanwhile, had started to find great success in the United States. Already citizens by birth, they entered professions such as law, politics, architecture, teaching, medicine, and business. Sometimes they faced racial hostility in the workplace, but attitudes were changing. By the 1970s, most Japanese American workers were well received, successful, and highly sought out by employers.

Many Japanese American college graduates enter professions such as law, medicine, and business.

The 1970s saw a new Japanese influx into the United States, but this time the "immigrants" were not people but businesses and consumer products. Japanese carmakers began selling small, fuel-efficient cars in the United States. Japanese electronics manufacturers sold televisions and stereo equipment. Some Americans resented the influx of Japanese-made goods into the U.S. market. They argued that by buying Japanese-made cars and other products, Americans were

Japanese and American businesses continue to form strong alliances. In this photo, the chairman and CEO of Sony (left) *and the chairman of AOL Time Warner* (right) *speak at an economic forum in New York City.*

hurting U.S. businesses. But the Japanese products were well made and low priced, and U.S. consumers rushed to buy them. Soon U.S. and Japanese manufacturers were making business deals. The United States and Japan, once bitter enemies, signed trade agreements. Japanese businesspeople frequently came to the United States for meetings, and Japanese tourists became common visitors to big U.S. cities.

Anti–Japanese sentiment faded into the background. Still, the old wounds of evacuation and relocation had not completely healed. Japanese Americans wanted the U.S. government to give a formal apology and more thorough compensation for their treatment during World War II.

The first step came in 1976, when U.S. president Gerald Ford signed a proclamation ending Executive Order 9066. (Although the law was no longer in use, it had never been officially ended.) The next step forward came with the Civil Liberties Act of 1988. This law ordered the Civil Rights Division of the U.S. Department of Justice to draw up a list of all former evacuees who were still alive on August 10, 1988, the day the law went into effect. Each person on the list got a check for $20,000 as compensation. After passage of the act, President Ronald Reagan formally apologized, on behalf of the U.S. government, to the former

President Ronald Reagan signs the Civil Liberties Act of 1988.

evacuees and their descendants. A man named
Mamoru Eto, aged 107, received the first
compensation check on October 9, 1990. Altogether,
approximately 62,500 Japanese Americans received
a total of $1.25 billion in payments.

Although many Japanese Americans had lost far
more in evacuation and relocation than they
recovered in redress payments, most former
evacuees and their descendants felt a sense of
victory with the passage of the 1988 act. To many,
the government's admission that evacuation was a
mistake meant a great deal. It affirmed the loyalty
of Japanese Americans during World War II and
formally rejected the notion that their ancestry

*U.S. attorney
general Dick
Thornburgh
presents the first
redress payments to
(from left to right)
Kisa Iseri, Hau
Dairiki, and
Mamoru Eto.*

made them somehow less American than their neighbors.

A New Century

At the beginning of the twenty-first century, the U.S. government took further steps to honor Japanese Americans of the World War II era. On July 21, 2000, the government awarded twenty-two Medals of Honor, the nation's highest military award, to Asian Americans who had served in World War II. Twenty of the medal recipients were members of the 442nd/100th combat unit.

President Clinton (right) *awards U.S. senator Daniel Inouye* (left) *a Congressional Medal of Honor on June 21, 2000. Inouye was a member of the 442nd Regimental Combat Team during World War II.*

Fifteen of those honored received their medals posthumously, or after death.

Later in the year, in November, the government dedicated (formally opened) the National Japanese American Memorial, located on the Mall in Washington, D.C. The memorial honors Japanese Americans who served in the military during World War II as well as those imprisoned in WRA camps.

Japanese Americans gather at the National Japanese American Memorial in Washington, D.C., for the dedication ceremony on November 9, 2000.

Its centerpiece is a fourteen-foot-high sculpture featuring two cranes—birds that are symbols of peace, long life, and good fortune in Japan.

Modern Japanese Americans are fully integrated into U.S. culture and society, and some Japanese Americans—especially young people—don't feel a strong connection to their Japanese ancestry. But many others have embraced their heritage. Some belong to Buddhist or Shinto temples. Others speak Japanese as well as English. Every year, Japanese Americans take part in many Japanese festivals, such as the Bon Festival, honoring the spirits of one's ancestors; the Japanese New Year; and the Tanabata Festival, which celebrates the meeting of two stars in the nighttime sky on July 7.

Nisei Week is a Los Angeles-area celebration that started in that city's Little Tokyo in 1934. Every year, except during World War II, Japanese Americans in Los Angeles have come together for the weeklong festival filled with parades, exhibits, dancing, and other events honoring their Japanese heritage. Craftspeople demonstrate Japanese floral arranging, calligraphy (ornamental

> *The family gets together and has a traditional breakfast. Then the female members of the family stay home and receive gifts from people who visit. My father was always going with the men, going from house to house to wish the families Happy New Year's. . . .*
> *It is a big holiday for Japanese families. Food is prepared for days on end.*
>
> —Kelly Hanzawa, the child of immigrants, describing her family's Japanese New Year celebration

Dancers in traditional Japanese dress perform in the Nisei Week parade in the Little Tokyo neighborhood of Los Angeles. Check out www.inamericabooks.com for links to locate Japanese events and activities in your area.

writing), and other traditional arts. Japanese martial (fighting) arts, tea ceremonies, and traditional costumes are also part of the celebration.

Thanks to television, the Internet, and high-speed travel, the distance between Japan and the United States seems shorter than ever. Japanese immigrants—several thousand a year—continue to move to the United States, only they travel by airplane instead of ship. These newcomers move to the United States for some of the same reasons earlier immigrants did—to study, to pursue business opportunities, or to marry

MY RACE IS A LINE THAT STRETCHES ACROSS OCEAN AND TIME TO LINK ME TO THE SHRINE WHERE MY GRANDMOTHER WAS RAISED.

—Kesaya E. Noda, a third-generation Japanese American

someone already living in the United States. Although moving to a new nation is never easy, modern Japanese immigrants do not face the same hardships and prejudices endured by the first generation of immigrants.

In fact, when new Japanese immigrants arrive in the United States, they are likely to see some familiar cultural landmarks. For instance, Japanese restaurants are commonplace in big U.S. cities. Americans love to eat sushi, a traditional Japanese dish consisting of rice dressed in vinegar, often topped with raw fish. It can also be rolled with seaweed and fish, egg, or vegetables. Tofu, a pressed white patty made from soybean milk, is another Japanese food that has earned many U.S. fans. Karaoke bars, which originated in Japan, are popular gathering places in the United States. At these bars, customers can take the stage and sing along to prerecorded music.

FROM GENERATION TO GENERATION

Each generation of Japanese Americans has a specific Japanese name. The word *issei* describes any person who was born in Japan but later moved to another country—a first-generation immigrant. A *nisei* is an immigrant's son or daughter who was born outside Japan. The third generation, the *sansei*, are the daughters and sons of the nisei. The *yonsei* are the fourth generation, and the *gosei* are the fifth generation. The term *Nikkei* refers to all Japanese Americans. It simply means "of Japanese descent."

KANI TO KYURI NO SUNOMONO
(CUCUMBER WITH CRAB)

This tasty side dish is a favorite among Japanese and Japanese Americans alike. To learn how to prepare other Japanese dishes, visit www.inamericabooks.com for links.

2 CUCUMBERS

1 TEASPOON SALT

6 OUNCES CANNED CRAB OR
    FROZEN CRAB, THAWED

SESAME SEEDS (OPTIONAL)

DRESSING:

$^1/_2$ CUP RICE VINEGAR

2 TABLESPOONS SUGAR

$^1/_4$ TEASPOON SOY SAUCE

1. Thinly slice cucumbers, place in bowl, and sprinkle with salt. Let stand for 5 minutes, then use your hands to gently squeeze water out of cucumbers.
2. Break crab into small pieces.
3. In another bowl, combine vinegar, sugar, and soy sauce to make dressing.
4. Put cucumber and crab in 4 small bowls and pour on dressing. Sprinkle with sesame seeds, if desired.

Serves 4

An example of anime popular in the United States, the Yu-Gi-Oh! franchise includes video games, trading cards, toys, a movie, and a cartoon. Yugi, from the animated movie Yu-Gi-Oh!, *is shown above.*

Anime is a fantastical style of animation that developed in Japan. The art form is extremely popular in the United States. Video and DVD rental shops often have several shelves devoted to anime movies. Manga, similar to anime, are Japanese comic books and cartoons. The Japanese martial arts—including aikido, judo, karate, and jujitsu—are also extremely popular in the United States. Japanese-made products continue to enjoy a large market in the United States. In addition to buying Japanese cars and electronics, Americans purchase Japanese-made video games and game players, trading cards, clothing, and decorative items.

JAPANESE MOVIES IN AMERICA

Japan has long exported its rich cultural offerings—including movies—to the United States. Akira Kurosawa was a famous Japanese film director whose movies are counted among the greatest in the world. One of his early films, *Rashomon*, won international acclaim in 1950. Several years later, Kurosawa's *The Seven Samurai* (1954) thrilled U.S. filmmakers and audiences. In fact, U.S. filmmakers remade the classic movie as a Western, *The Magnificent Seven*, in 1960.

Another Japanese film that wowed U.S. audiences was *Godzilla*, released in Japan in 1954 and followed by many popular sequels. The original Godzilla movies are still wildly popular with U.S. audiences.

Hayao Miyazaki's animated films, such as *Princess Mononoke*, *Spirited Away*, and *Howl's Moving Castle*, are popular in the United States as well. *Spirited Away* won the 2003 Oscar for Best Animated Feature.

Also increasingly popular are remakes of Japanese horror films. *The Ring*, based on the Japanese film *Ringu*, was released in 2002. *The Grudge* (based on the Ju-On series of films in Japan) was released in 2004. It was so popular that a sequel is in the works.

> *I would urge the younger generations [of Japanese Americans] to hold onto whatever heritage they were raised with, and if they weren't raised with any, to reach back and find it in their families. . . . And I believe firmly that my life is so much richer for embracing my Japanese side, and I want other [Japanese Americans] to dig a little deeper for their own roots. . . . Now, I realize that even the farthest branches are always connected to the tree.*
>
> —Gil Asakawa, Japanese American author

Japan and the United States were once enemies, and Japanese Americans were caught in the middle. In modern times, Japan and the United States are allies and trading partners. The two nations engage in a rich cultural exchange. In some ways, Japanese Americans still occupy a middle ground between the two cultures, but that middle ground is more of a bridge than a dividing line. As the new century goes on, that bridge will certainly only grow stronger.

FAMOUS JAPANESE AMERICANS

KEIKO AGENA (b. 1973) Agena is well known to fans of the TV series *Gilmore Girls*. Agena plays Lane Kim,  a brainy and offbeat friend of the show's lead character, Rory Gilmore. Born in Honolulu, Hawaii, Agena took up acting at the age of ten. She briefly studied drama at Whitman College in Washington State before moving to Hollywood to pursue an acting career. She has played parts in movies and TV shows, including *Felicity*, *Law and Order*, *ER*, and *Beverly Hills 90210*. In addition to appearing on camera, Agena works with a Los Angeles–based Asian American theater company called hereandnow.

DEVON AOKI (b. 1982) Supermodel and actor Devon Aoki was born in New York, New York. Her father is Rocky Aoki, founder of the successful Benihana Japanese restaurant chain. Aoki began her modeling career as a teenager. She has walked the runway for top  clothing designers, and photos of her have appeared in magazines such as *Interview* and *Visionaire*. In 2003 she made her first feature film, *The Fast and the Furious 2*. In 2005 she appeared in *Sin City*, a dark crime movie.

ANN CURRY (b. 1956) A native of Ashland, Oregon, Ann Curry is a news anchor on the popular NBC *Today* show. As a young woman, Curry studied journalism at the University of Oregon. After graduation, she worked as a reporter and news anchor for television stations in Oregon; Los Angeles, California; and Chicago, Illinois. Curry became the *Today*  show news anchor in 1997. She lives in New York City.

JAMES IHA (b. 1968) Born in Chicago, Illinois, James Iha came to fame as a founder of the rock band Smashing Pumpkins. The band formed in 1988. It produced several albums and won widespread acclaim

before breaking up in 2000. Iha, a guitarist, has since joined a new band, A Perfect Circle, and has released a solo album. Iha lives in New York City, where he owns an independent record label called Scratchie Records.

MICHIO KAKU (b. 1947) Kaku, a

physicist and author, is a leader in a branch of physics called superstring theory. Born in San Francisco, California, Kaku attended Harvard University as an undergraduate and earned his Ph.D. from the University of California, Berkeley. For more than twenty-five years, Kaku has taught theoretical physics at the City University of New York. He is the author of nine books, including *Hyperspace: A Scientific Odyssey through Parallel Universes, Time Warps, and the 10th Dimension*. He also hosts a weekly radio show called *Explorations*. Kaku's parents were among the thousands of Japanese Americans imprisoned during World War II.

NORMAN MINETA (b. 1931)

Secretary of Transportation Norman Mineta was born in San Jose, California. During World War II, he and his family were imprisoned along with other Americans of Japanese descent. As a young man, Mineta attended the University of California in Berkeley and then served in the U.S. Army. From 1975 to 1995, Mineta served as a U.S. congressional representative from California. He then served as secretary of commerce during the presidency of Bill Clinton. President George W. Bush named Mineta U.S. secretary of transportation in 2001. In this position, he heads the U.S. Department of Transportation, which overseas the

nation's roads, natural gas pipelines, railroads, waterways, airports, and public transportation systems.

PATSY MINK (1927–2002) Patsy

Mink was the first woman of Asian descent to serve in the U.S. Congress. Born in Paia on the island of Maui in Hawaii, Mink faced racism during World War II, but she and her fellow Japanese Hawaiians were not sent to

relocation camps. After the war, Mink attended the University of Hawaii and then the University of Nebraska. She studied law at the University of Chicago, earning her law degree in 1951. In 1956 she won election to Hawaii's territorial legislature, and in 1965 she was elected to the U.S. House of Representatives. She served in the House until 1977 and served again from 1990 until her death in 2002. During her years in office, Mink frequently fought for legislation to benefit women, children, and minorities.

KEN MOCHIZUKI (b. 1954)

Mochizuki is an acclaimed children's book author born in Seattle. He has written three picture books. *How Baseball Saved Us* (1993) tells of a Japanese American boy sent to a relocation camp during World War II. *Heroes* (1997) features a young boy coming to understand his Japanese American heritage in the 1960s. *Passage to Freedom: The Sugihara Story* tells the true story of a Japanese diplomat who helped save thousands of Polish Jews from death during World War II. Mochizuki has also written a young adult novel, *Beacon Hill Boys* (2002), which examines the lives of four modern-day Japanese American teenagers. He attended the University of Washington in Seattle, where he still makes his home.

JOHNNIE MORTON (b. 1971)

Wide receiver Johnnie Morton plays professional football for the Kansas City Chiefs. Morton was born in Torrance, California, and attended college at the University of Southern California. He played for eight seasons with the Detroit Lions before signing on with Kansas City in 2002. His brother Chad is also a professional football player. Chad plays for the Washington Redskins.

HIKARU NAKAMURA (b. 1987)

Nakamura is a chess prodigy who became an American grandmaster (the ranking for a chess player) at the age of fifteen. Born in Hirakata City, Japan, Nakamura moved to the United States with his family at the

age of two. He began playing chess at the age of seven and immediately began winning youth chess tournaments. By the age of ten, he was playing in and winning adult tournaments. Rated among the top chess players in the world, Nakamura lives in White Plains, New York.

ISAMU NOGUCHI (1904–1988)

Noguchi, a world-famous sculptor,

was born in Los Angeles, California. He attended Columbia University in New York and then studied sculpture in Paris. In addition to sculptural works, Noguchi created stage sets and furniture. One of his best-known works is a relief sculpture designed for the Associated Press Building in New York City. In 1964 Noguchi served as a consultant for the design of John F. Kennedy's tomb in Arlington National Cemetery in Arlington, Virginia. Through the course of his career, he exhibited works in nearly every major art museum in the United States.

HIDEO NOMO (b. 1968)

Nomo, the first Japanese baseball player ever to pitch in the American major leagues, plays baseball with the Tampa Bay Devil Rays. A native of Osaka, Japan, Nomo began his career as a member of Japan's national baseball team. There, he earned the nickname the Tornado for his distinctive pitching style, which involves twisting his body. Nomo joined the Los Angeles Dodgers in 1995 and was named 1995 National League Rookie of the Year. He joined the Devil Rays in 2005.

APOLO ANTON OHNO (b. 1982)

Speed skater Apolo Ohno began skating in 1994 and quickly moved to the top of the U.S. junior speed skating circuit. He made a splash at the 2002 Winter Olympics in Salt Lake City, Utah, winning a gold medal in the 1,500-meter race and a silver in the 1,000. His hip, flashy personal style won him—and speed skating—many new fans. Ohno was born in Seattle, Washington. He makes his home in Colorado Springs, Colorado.

ELLISON ONIZUKA (1946–1986)

Onizuka, the first Japanese

American to travel in space, was born in Kealakekua, Hawaii. After earning degrees in aerospace engineering from the University of Colorado, Onizuka joined the National Aeronautics and Space Administration (NASA) in 1978. His first space flight came in 1985, when he took part in a military mission aboard the space shuttle *Discovery*. The following year, tragedy struck: The space shuttle *Challenger* exploded shortly after takeoff from the Kennedy Space Center in Florida. Onizuka and six other astronauts were killed in the explosion.

YOKO ONO (b. 1933) A musician

and artist, Ono was born in Tokyo. Her father was a banker who did business in the United States, and the whole family moved to New York in 1951. After attending Sarah Lawrence College, Ono became a visual artist, famous for working with unconventional materials and subjects. She met John Lennon, a member of the rock band the Beatles, whom she married in 1969. Ono and

Lennon became well known for their musical collaborations but even more for their efforts to protest the Vietnam War and promote world peace. Lennon was murdered in 1980. Ono continues to record music, create art, and work for peace.

SEIJI OZAWA (b. 1935) One of the

most accomplished symphony conductors in the world, Ozawa was born to Japanese parents in Shenyang, China. As a young man, he studied music in Tokyo. He then moved to Germany to study conducting. Leonard Bernstein of the New York Philharmonic Orchestra saw Ozawa in Europe and, impressed by Ozawa's abilities, named him assistant conductor of the New York Philharmonic for

the 1961–62 season. From 1965 to 1969, Ozawa conducted the Toronto Symphony, and in 1968 he was named conductor and musical director of the San Francisco Symphony Orchestra. From 1973 to 2002, he directed the Boston Symphony Orchestra, then took the job of music director for the Vienna State Opera.

ERIC SHINSEKI (b. 1942) Eric Shinseki served as chief of staff of the U.S. Army, the army's top job, from 1999 to 2003. A native of Lihue, Kauai, in Hawaii, Shinseki graduated from the U.S. Military Academy in 1965 and then pursued a full-time army career. He was wounded in the Vietnam War. He later served in officer positions around the United States and overseas, eventually becoming a general. Shinseki retired from the army in 2003, right at the start of the Iraq war.

GEORGE TAKEI (b. 1937) Takei is most famous for playing the role of Sulu on the first *Star Trek* television series and in six Star Trek films. Takei was born in Los Angeles, California, and along with his family was imprisoned at two WRA camps

after the attack on Pearl Harbor. He studied architecture at the University of California in Berkeley before switching to acting in the mid–1950s. In addition to his Star Trek performances, Takei has appeared in countless other films, TV shows, and plays during his long career. His 1994 autobiography, *To the Stars*, chronicles his experiences in relocation camps as well as his success in acting.

KRISTI YAMAGUCHI (b. 1971) Olympic champion Kristi Yamaguchi was born in Fremont, California. She took up ice skating as a young girl and quickly moved to the top of the junior figure  skating world, then to the top of adult competition. She has won numerous skating honors, including a gold medal at the 1992 Olympic Games in Albertville, France. In 1996 Yamaguchi established the Always Dream Foundation, an organization dedicated to helping children. Yamaguchi was named to the U.S. Figure Skating Hall of Fame in 1998.

TIMELINE

A.D. 600s   Kotoku becomes Japan's first emperor.

1180s   The Minamoto clan sets up a military-style government
               in Kamakura, Japan. The head of the clan, Yoritomo,
               becomes the nation's first shogun, or military leader.

1549   Francis Xavier, a Portuguese priest, arrives in Japan on a
               mission to convert Japanese people to Christianity.

1603   Tokugawa Ieyasu becomes shogun.

1630s   Tokugawa Ieyasu expels most foreigners from Japan.

1853   U.S. naval officer Matthew Perry arrives in Japan to
               demand ties between Japan and the United States.

1854   Japan and the United States sign the Treaty of Kanagawa,
               establishing diplomatic relations between the two nations.

1858   Japan and the United States sign a trade agreement.

1866   The Japanese government allows citizens to travel
               abroad legally.

1867   Japanese military leaders overthrow the Tokugawa
               Shogunate and set up the Meiji government.

1900   The Hawaiian Islands become a U.S. territory.

1904   Japan goes to war with Russia.

1905   The Japanese Association of America is established in
               San Francisco.

1906   An earthquake hits San Francisco, followed by a wave of
               anti-Japanese sentiment.

1908   Japan and the United States make the Gentlemen's

Agreement, severely limiting Japanese immigration to the United States.

1913   California passes the Alien Land Law, prohibiting noncitizens from buying land in California.

1921   Washington State passes a law prohibiting land ownership by Japanese Americans. Japan agrees to stop picture–bride immigration to the United States.

1924   The U.S. Congress passes the Immigration Act of 1924, barring immigration by anyone who is ineligible for U.S. citizenship.

1931   Japan invades Manchuria, a province of China.

1937   Japan begins a war with China.

1939   World War II begins in Europe.

1940   Japan joins the Axis powers and invades French Indochina.

1941   Japan bombs Pearl Harbor, Hawaii, leading to U.S. entry into World War II.

1942   President Franklin Roosevelt signs Executive Order 9066, authorizing the removal of Japanese Americans from the West Coast. More than 110,000 Japanese Americans must leave their homes for relocation camps.

1943   The U.S. government allows Japanese men to join the 442nd Regimental Combat Team, an all–Japanese American unit.

1944   The 442nd Regimental Combat Team merges with the 100th Infantry Battalion, another Japanese American combat unit. The Supreme Court rules that the evacuation and relocation of loyal U.S. citizens is illegal.

1945	The relocation camps are shut down. Japan surrenders to the United States, ending World War II.
1948	Congress awards citizenship to any aliens who served in the U.S. military during World War II, including members of the 100th and 442nd combat units. Congress passes the Evacuation Claims Act, authorizing compensation to Japanese Americans for wartime losses.
1952	The McCarran–Walter Act eliminates race as a consideration for U.S. citizenship, allowing thousands of Asians to become citizens.
1959	Hawaii becomes the fiftieth state in the United States. Its congressional representative, Daniel Inouye, becomes the first Japanese American in the U.S. Congress.
1976	President Gerald Ford officially ends Executive Order 9066.
1988	The Civil Liberties Act authorizes payments of twenty thousand dollars each to former evacuees.
2000	The U.S. government awards twenty–two Medals of Honor to Asian American World War II veterans, most of them members of the 442nd/100th combat unit. The National Japanese American Memorial opens on the Mall in Washington, D.C.
2002	Japanese Americans mark the sixtieth anniversary of the signing of Executive Order 9066.
2005	U.S. and Japanese peace activists mark the sixtieth anniversary of the dropping of atomic bombs on Japan during World War II.

GLOSSARY

ALIEN: a noncitizen

BOYCOTT: to refuse to do business with a person, group of people, business, or government

EVACUATION: the removal of people from a certain area, such as a military zone

INTEGRATED: absorbed into the mainstream culture

INTERNMENT: confinement of a group of people, especially during wartime

IRRIGATION: a system for carrying water to crops, using pipes, pumps, and other devices

RELOCATION: settlement in a new place

SEGREGATION: the forced separation of people of different racial or ethnic groups

SHOGUNATE: a military government operating in Japan from the late 1100s to 1867

WESTERN: relating to non–Asian cultures, especially those of the United States and Western Europe

THINGS TO SEE AND DO

ANGEL ISLAND IMMIGRATION STATION, SAN FRANCISCO, CALIFORNIA
http://www.angelisland.org/immigr02.html
The Angel Island Immigration Station, located on an island in San Francisco Bay, opened in 1910 to process immigrants arriving in the United States from Asia. During the next thirty years, thousands of Asian immigrants passed through the station. Most were from China, but some were from Japan. Thousands of Japanese picture brides passed through the station before meeting their new husbands in the United States. The station was shut down after World War II but reopened as a museum later in the century.

JAPANESE AMERICAN NATIONAL MUSEUM, LOS ANGELES, CALIFORNIA
http://www.janm.org
This museum in Los Angeles offers exhibits on the Japanese American experience. Past exhibits have dealt with Japanese history, the lives of early immigrants, the Japanese in Hawaii, and Japanese American artists. The museum also hosts workshops and educational programs that will interest Japanese Americans and non–Japanese Americans alike.

MANZANAR NATIONAL HISTORIC SITE, INDEPENDENCE, CALIFORNIA
http://www.nps.gov/manz
Located at the base of the Sierra Nevada in eastern California, Manzanar is the best preserved of the ten World War II–era relocation camps. Operated by the National Park Service, the modern–day site offers exhibits, films, and books about evacuation and relocation. Visitors can also tour the ruins of camp buildings and facilities.

NATIONAL CHERRY BLOSSOM FESTIVAL, WASHINGTON, D.C.
http://www.nationalcherryblossomfestival.org
In 1912 the city of Tokyo, Japan, gave a gift of three thousand cherry trees to the people of Washington, D.C. Every year, Washington celebrates the gift with its National Cherry Blossom Festival, a celebration of Japanese culture, cherry blossoms, and international friendship. Held in late March and early April, when the cherry trees bloom, the festival includes a parade, a street fair, Japanese foods and music, and educational events.

NATIONAL JAPANESE AMERICAN MEMORIAL, WASHINGTON, D.C.
http://www.njamf.com
Dedicated in November 2000, the memorial honors the loyalty and courage of Japanese Americans during World War II. It commemorates the heroism and sacrifice of Japanese Americans who fought in the U.S. military during the war, as well as the suffering of more than 110,000 men, women, and children who endured evacuation and relocation. Located on the Mall in Washington, D.C., the memorial includes a central crane sculpture and surrounding inscribed panels that tell the story.

SOURCE NOTES

14 Dorothy Hoobler and Thomas Hoobler, *The Japanese American Family Album* (New York: Oxford University Press, 1996), 21.

18 Yuji Ichioka, *The Issei: The World of the First Generation Japanese Immigrants, 1885–1924.* (New York: Free Press, 1988), 83.

21 Hoobler and Hoobler, 38.

25 Ronald Takaki, *Strangers from a Different Shore: A History of Asian Americans* (Boston: Little, Brown and Company, 1989), 179.

34 Page Smith, *Democracy on Trial: The Japanese American Evacuation and Relocation in World War II* (New York: Simon and Schuster, 1995), 107.

35 Ibid., 117.

36 Ibid., 126–127.

37 Ibid., 146.

38 Ibid., 245.

46 "The National Japanese American Memorial Inscriptions," *National Japanese American Memorial Foundation,* January 26, 2000, http://www.njamf.com/quotes.htm (May 17, 2005).

55 Hoobler and Hoobler, 114.

56 Ibid., 116.

61 Gil Asakawa, "Roots and Branches: Who's Japanese American?" *IM Diversity.com,* April 28, 2003, http://www.imdiversity.com/Villages/Asian/history_heritage/archives/asakawa_roots_and_branches.asp (April 5, 2005).

SELECTED BIBLIOGRAPHY

Asakawa, Gil. *Being Japanese American: A JA Sourcebook for Nikkei, Hapa . . . and Their Friends.* Albany, CA: Stone Bridge Press, 2004. **The author, a third-generation Japanese American, examines what it means to be Japanese American in the twenty-first century. Using interviews with fellow Japanese Americans, Asakawa reveals a multifaceted community that has embraced both its heritage and its future. He also explores the experiences of the hapa—a nickname for people of mixed Asian and Caucasian heritage.**

Hoobler, Dorothy, and Thomas Hoobler. *The Japanese American Family Album.* New York: Oxford University Press, 1996. **Organized chronologically, this book follows the Japanese American experience across more than one hundred years. The authors draw on oral histories and archival documents to trace the journey from Japan to the United States, from the late 1800s into the 1990s.**

Ichioka, Yuji. *The Issei: The World of the First Generation Japanese Immigrants, 1885–1924.* New York: Free Press, 1988. **This comprehensive title examines the lives and experiences of the issei, or first-generation Japanese immigrants—from immigration and settlement to labor struggles and legal battles.**

Japanese American National Museum. *Encyclopedia of Japanese American History: An A-to-Z Reference from 1868 to the Present.* New York: Facts on File, 2000. **This thorough reference book includes statistics, history, alphabetical entries, and suggestions for further reading on the topic of the Japanese in America.**

Kurashige, Lon. *Japanese American Celebration and Conflict: A History of Ethnic Identity and Festival, 1934–1990.* Berkeley: University of California Press, 2002. **This scholarly work examines the Japanese American community and how it has—and has not—integrated into the U.S. mainstream.**

Smith, Page. *Democracy on Trial: The Japanese American Evacuation and Relocation in World War II.* New York:

Simon and Schuster, 1995. **This comprehensive book recounts the history of Japanese immigration to the United States and explores World War II evacuation and relocation in great detail. The author cites U.S. government documents as well as interviews with evacuees to present a thorough picture of the Japanese American experience in World War II.**

Takaki, Ronald. *Strangers from a Different Shore: A History of Asian Americans.* Boston: Little, Brown and Company, 1989. **This work examines the experiences of various Asian groups in the United States, including Chinese, Japanese, Filipinos, East Indians, Koreans,** and Vietnamese. **It includes sections devoted specifically to the Japanese American experience, with a lengthy discussion of Japanese American evacuation and relocation.**

Wilson, Robert A., and Bill Hosokawa. *East to America: A History of the Japanese in the United States.* New York: Quill, 1982. **This book offers a detailed look at the Japanese American experience. It examines the lives of nineteenth-century Japanese immigrants, the growth of immigrant communities, and the World War II era. It also explores postwar legal victories and efforts to redress the injustices endured by Japanese Americans during the war.**

FURTHER READING & WEBSITES

NONFICTION

Behnke, Alison. *Japan in Pictures.* Minneapolis: Lerner Publications Company, 2003. **This comprehensive title introduces readers to Japanese history, government, and society. By exploring Japanese culture, the book helps shed light on the Japanese American experience.**

California Historical Society. *Only What We Could Carry: The Japanese American Internment Experience.* Berkeley, CA: Heyday Books, 2000. **Using poetry, fiction, news stories, government documents, photographs, drawings, and cartoons, this book presents a thorough picture of Japanese American evacuation and relocation.**

Most moving are the diary entries, letters, and other writings of the evacuees themselves.

Hamanaka, Sheila. *Journey: Japanese Americans, Racism, and Renewal*. New York: Orchard Books, 1990. This book is based on the author's extraordinary twenty-five-foot mural that depicts the Japanese American experience, with emphasis on evacuation and relocation. Close-ups of the mural are accompanied by vivid, moving text.

Stanley, Jerry. *I Am an American: A True Story of Japanese Internment*. New York: Crown Books for Young Readers, 1996. This well-researched volume documents the World War II evacuation and relocation experience in great detail. Stark black-and-white photos help convey the suffering of evacuees.

Welch, Catherine. *Children of the Relocation Camps*. Minneapolis: Carolrhoda Books, 2000. Using historical photographs and quotations, Welch paints a vivid picture of the World War II evacuation and relocation experience of Japanese American children.

Weston, Reiko. *Cooking the Japanese Way*. Minneapolis: Lerner Publications Company, 2002. Readers can explore Japanese culture by learning to cook easy-to-make Japanese meals. In addition to recipes, the book also includes information about Japanese festivals and holidays.

Whitman, Sylvia. *V Is for Victory: The American Home Front during World War II*. Minneapolis: Lerner Publications Company, 1993. Whitman examines World War II on the home front in the United States. The book includes photos and stories of Japanese Americans forced into relocation camps.

FICTION

Kadohata, Cynthia. *Kira-Kira*. New York: Atheneum, 2004. Winner of the Newbery Medal as the most distinguished American children's book in 2004, this novel for young readers tells the story of the Japanese American Takeshima family. The narrator is Katie Takeshima, a young girl growing up in the 1950s. When her sister, Lynn, becomes dreadfully ill, Katie's world turns upside down.

Uchida, Yoshiko. *Journey to Topaz.* Reprint edition. Berkeley, CA: Heyday Books, 2004. Eleven-year-old Yuki lives in the bleak and dusty Topaz relocation camp with her family. This book, originally published in 1971, traces her joys, struggles, and sadness. The author has based the story on her own childhood experiences at the Topaz camp in Utah.

WEBSITES

INAMERICABOOKS.COM
http://www.inamericabooks.com
Visit www.inamericabooks.com, the online home of the In America series, to get linked to all sorts of useful information. You'll find historical and cultural websites related to individual groups, as well as general information on genealogy, creating your own family tree, and the history of immigration in America.

JAPANESE AMERICAN CITIZENS LEAGUE
http://www.jacl.org
The Japanese American Citizens League is dedicated to preserving the rights and liberties of Japanese Americans and all other victims of injustice. The website includes news of interest to the Japanese American community, educational information, and links to other organizations.

NATIONAL JAPANESE AMERICAN HISTORICAL SOCIETY
http://www.njahs.org
Based in San Francisco, the National Japanese American Historical Society is dedicated to preserving and promoting the history and culture of Japanese Americans. On the website, readers can learn about NJAHS exhibits and special programs and find links to related organizations.

INDEX

ACKNOWLEDGMENTS: THE PHOTOGRAPHS IN THIS BOOK ARE REPRODUCED WITH THE PERMISSION OF: © Digital Vision Royalty Free, pp. 1, 3, 22; © A.A.M. Van der Heyden/Independent Picture Service, p. 6; © The Art Archive, p. 7; © The Art Archive/Rijksmuseum voor Volkenkunde Leiden (Leyden)/Dagli Orti, p. 8; Library of Congress, pp. 10 (LC–USZC4–3379), 12 (LC–USZC2–723), 13 (LC–D4–43120); Hawaii Visitors Bureau, p. 18; courtesy of Toyo Miyatake, p. 23; Gift of Grace Ito, Mary Nakasuji and Helen Shintaku, Japanese American National Museum, p. 24; National Archives, pp. 27 (NWDNS–111–AG–9), 32 (NWDNS–80–G–32420), 33, 35 (NWDNS–210–G–2A–35), 39 (NWDNS–210–G–B716), 45 (NWDNS–210–G–14–R–1), 47; Smithsonian, National Museum of American History (BA–I–1), p. 28; U.S. Army, pp. 37, 41; St. Paul Dispatch & Pioneer Press/Minnesota Historical Society, p. 40; photo by Paul J. Buklarewicz, p. 49; © Reuters/CORBIS, p. 50; courtesy Ronald Reagan Library, p. 51; AP/Wide World Photos, p. 52; GEORGE BRIDGES/AFP/Getty Images, p. 53; HIROKO MASUIKE/AFP/Getty Images, 54; © Joseph Sohm; ChromoSohm Inc./CORBIS, p. 56; © Courtesy of Warner Bros/Bureau L.A. Collections/ CORBIS, p. 59; © Glenn Weiner/ZUMA Press, p. 62 (left); © Jeff Frank– KPA/ZUMA KPA, p. 62 (top right); © Dan Herrick–KPA/ZUMA Press, p. 62 (bottom right); © Mitchell Gerber/CORBIS, p. 63 (left); U.S. Department of Transportation, p. 63 (right); courtesy Congresswoman Patsy T. Mink, p. 64 (left); John Henderson, America's Foundation for Chess, p. 64 (right); © Nathan Benn/CORBIS, p. 65 (left); © Mike Carlson/Icon SMI/ZUMA Press, p. 65 (top right); © Debbie Van Story– KPA/Keystone Pictures/ZUMA Press, p. 65 (bottom right); NASA, p. 66 (left); © Livio Valerio/La Presse/ZUMA Press, p. 66 (top right); © Bela Benko/PPS Vienna/ZUMA Press, p. 66 (bottom right); © Laura Farr/ZUMA Press, p. 67, Maps by Bill Hauser, pp. 11, 30.

Cover photo: © Bettmann/CORBIS (main); © A.A.M. Van der Heyden/ Independent Picture Service (bottom); © Digital Vision Royalty Free (title, back cover).

DISCARD